Contents

Any words appearing in the text in bold,
like this, are explained in the Glossary.

What is a rock?

What do Mount St Helens in the state of Washington, USA and the sandy shores of Raasay in Scotland, have in common with a gravestone and some ancient Native American tools? They are all made of igneous rock.

Igneous rock is one of three groups of rocks found in the world. The other two groups are **sedimentary rock** and **metamorphic rock**. Each kind of rock forms in a different way. Examples of igneous rock include granite, gabbro, basalt, obsidian, pumice and tuff.

Many gravestones are made of granite. It is cheaper and easier to quarry than slate, a common gravestone rock in the past.

Rocks are all around you. They are under your feet and at the top of the highest mountains. They are in buildings and on riverbeds. Rocks come in all shapes and sizes. You can see tiny pebbles on the beach or along the side of the road. You can see giant boulders at a local park or in the woods.

DID YOU KNOW?

Basalt is a common igneous rock. It is one of the heaviest and densest rocks on the Earth.

All three kinds of rock are made of **minerals**. A mineral is a natural solid material. It always has the same chemical makeup and the same structure. This means that the **atoms** that mix together to form a mineral always arrange themselves in the same way.

Geologists, who study the Earth, and petrologists – scientists who study rocks – can identify a rock by knowing where it came from and by looking at the **properties** of its minerals. They examine the colour, shininess and hardness of the minerals. They also study the size, shape and arrangement of the crystals.

A crystal structure

Most minerals have a **crystal** structure. Crystals usually have a regular shape and smooth, flat sides called **faces**. Quartz, the most common mineral, is an example of a mineral sometimes found in igneous rock. The crystal structure of quartz is made up of silicon and oxygen atoms that are always arranged in the same way. Quartz crystals always have six faces and are often used in glassmaking and in jewellery.

Rhyolite is a light-coloured igneous rock that contains the same minerals as granite. These rhyolite boulders are in a riverbed in Mexico.

Layers of the Earth

The Earth is a giant ball of rock. The layer of rock that you walk on every day is called the **crust**. Below the Earth's crust is a much thicker layer called the **mantle**. The mantle is made of hot, soft rock in a liquid state, known as **magma**. Like porridge, magma is thick, but it can flow.

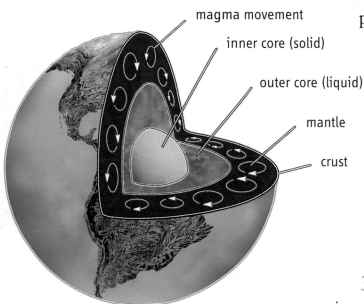

magma movement

inner core (solid)

outer core (liquid)

mantle

crust

The Earth is made up of layers. The thin, outer layer of the Earth is the crust. The next layer, the mantle, is made of magma that is constantly moving. The core is made of an outer liquid layer and an inner solid core.

The core

The Earth's sizzling-hot **core** has two parts. The temperature of the melted metals that make up the outer core is at least 3700°C. The inner core is even hotter, but it is made of solid metals. The weight of all the other layers presses down on the inner core, creating enormous pressure. That pressure holds the **molecules** that make up the

DID YOU KNOW?

When the Earth formed 4.6 billion years ago, the entire planet was made of molten magma. It took millions of years for the Earth to cool enough for its crust to solidify.

THAT'S INCREDIBLE!

You might wonder how scientists found out that the Earth has three layers. After all, no one can travel to the centre of our planet. It's much too hot.

Many years ago, seismologists – scientists who study earthquakes – noticed that waves of energy travel through the Earth during, and just after, an earthquake. After carefully measuring the energy waves, seismologists realized that the waves speed up, slow down and change direction as they zoom through the planet.

At first, scientists had trouble explaining these changes. Eventually, however, they decided that the movement of energy waves indicates that different parts of the Earth's interior are made of different materials. In recent years, seismologists have studied earthquake waves to calculate how thick each layer is and to determine the makeup of each layer.

inner core very close together. They are so close that they cannot turn into a liquid, in spite of the high temperature.

Energy flow

Just as heat from a mug of hot cocoa can transfer itself to your hands as you hold it, heat is always moving upwards from the Earth's core into the cooler mantle. This flow of heat energy causes magma in the Earth's mantle to slowly swirl in giant circles. As the hottest magma moves toward the Earth's surface, cooler magma moves back down to take its place.

Land on the move

Have you ever looked closely at an ice cube floating in a glass of water? Ice is less dense than liquid water, so a little bit of the ice always sticks above the water's surface. In some ways, the Earth's **crust** has a lot in common with the ice in a glass of water. The crust is broken into giant pieces called **tectonic plates**. Each plate floats on top of the **magma** in the **mantle**. The land and oceans are the top part top of the crust.

Moving plates

As heat from the Earth's **core** moves upwards and forces magma to move, the Earth's plates move, too. In some parts of the world, plates move apart, and long cracks called **rifts** are left behind. When rifts form under the ocean, the material from the mantle rises to the surface and creates new land on either side of the rift. This process is called **seafloor spreading**. As magma

The Earth's surface is broken into many plates. The major plates are labelled on this diagram. The plates are moving constantly, though very slowly, in the direction of the arrows. The Mid-Atlantic Ridge is a rift formed by two plates moving apart.

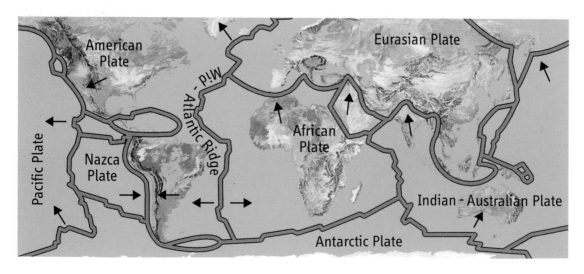

American Plate

Eurasian Plate

Mid-Atlantic Ridge

Pacific Plate

Nazca Plate

African Plate

Indian - Australian Plate

Antarctic Plate

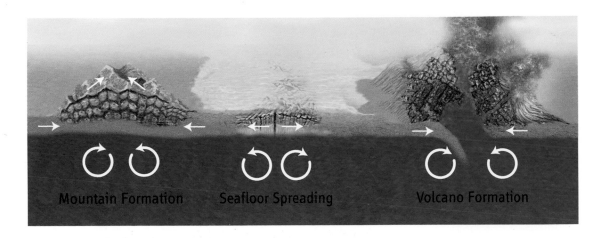

Mountain Formation   Seafloor Spreading   Volcano Formation

from inside the Earth seeps through the Mid-Atlantic Ridge, it creates new seabed. That is why North America and Europe are slowly moving apart and the Atlantic Ocean is getting bigger.

Making mountains

In other parts of the world, plates bump into one another. Sometimes one plate slides over the other. Then the bottom plate moves down into the mantle where it melts. When two plates hit head-on and push against each other with great force, the land buckles and tall mountains form. When two plates scrape past each other, the result is a **transform fault**, such as the San Andreas Fault in California or the Dead Sea Fault in the Middle East. When enough pressure builds up along faults like these, an earthquake occurs.

Mountains may form when two plates hit head-on. The seabed expands as magma rises through a rift. When one plate moves below another, magma may rise to the surface and escape through a **volcano**.

WHAT A DISCOVERY!

In 1912, a German scientist named Alfred Wegner noticed that some of the continents seem to fit together like the pieces of a jigsaw puzzle. He suggested that the Earth's crust is made of moving plates. Scientists couldn't imagine what would cause land to move, so they did not accept Wegner's theory. Now we know that Wegner was right. At one time, all the land on the Earth formed a single continent, known as Pangaea.

Three groups of rocks

Gabbro is one example of igneous rock. It is heavy and, usually, is a greenish colour.

Sandstone is a sedimentary rock that forms as sand is pressed together over millions of years. Its colour is determined by the material that binds the sand together.

The Earth has three major groups of rocks – igneous, **sedimentary**, and **metamorphic**. Each kind of rock forms in a different way.

Igneous rocks form when **magma** from the Earth's **mantle** cools and forms crystals. Granite, basalt, pumice, rhyolite, andesite and gabbro are all examples of igneous rocks.

Sedimentary rocks form as layers of mud, clay, sand and other materials build up over time. The weight of the materials at the top of the pile presses down on the materials below. All that pressure cements the materials together to form rock. If you look closely at sedimentary rocks, you may be able to see the layers. Limestone, sandstone, shale, breccia and conglomerate are all examples of sedimentary rocks.

Metamorphic rocks form when heat or pressure changes the **minerals** that make up igneous rocks, sedimentary rocks or another metamorphic rocks. This often happens when the Earth's **tectonic plates** collide and push up tall mountain ranges. As India crashes into the rest of Asia, the

THE MOST COMMON ROCK

Although sedimentary rock is the rock most commonly exposed on the Earth's surface, most of our planet's crust is actually made of igneous rock. Many mountains are made of igneous rock. They form as lava spills out of the crust, cools, solidifies and slowly piles up.

Himalaya Mountains – the tallest mountains on the Earth – slowly rise into the sky. Millions of years ago, the Appalachian Mountains in North America and the Caledonian mountain range in Scotland and Norway formed in the same way. Metamorphic rock also forms when a stream of magma bursts into the **crust** and cooks surrounding rock. Marble, slate, schist, gneiss, hornfels and serpentinite are examples of metamorphic rock.

The metamorphic rock schist is one of the toughest rocks on the Earth. The pattern of minerals in this rock resembles wood grain.

DID YOU KNOW?

The word 'igneous' comes from a Latin term meaning 'made from fire'. Of course, igneous rock is not really made from fire, but the Earth's inner heat does play an important role in moving the liquid magma to places where it can cool and become solid igneous rock.

A look at volcanoes

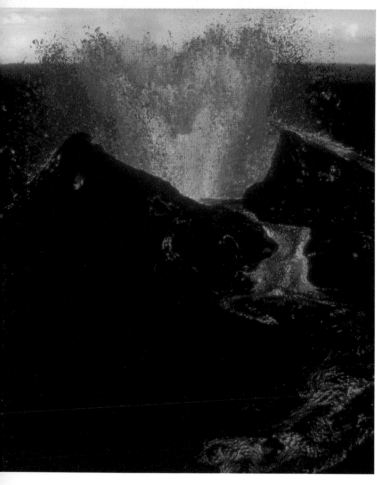

Kilauea in Hawaii is the world's most active volcano. There is an observatory on the rim of its crater.

A **volcano** is a crack or hole in the Earth's surface that extends through the **crust** and into the **mantle**. Some people also use the word volcano to describe the large mountain-like mound that builds up around the opening over time. Most volcanoes form in places where the Earth's **tectonic plates** meet. So many volcanoes rise along the edges of the Pacific Plate that this area is sometimes called the 'Ring of Fire'.

The lava that spews from volcanoes is **magma** that has moved upwards from the Earth's mantle. When lava hits air or water, it starts to cool immediately. In a few days or weeks, the lava hardens and becomes igneous rock, such as basalt. If you look closely at some rocks, you can see their **crystals**. But the **minerals** that make up basalt cool so quickly that they have no time to form visible crystals.

There are about 500 active volcanoes in the world today. When a volcano erupts, a grey cloud of ash fills the air, and lava flows out of the volcano. Scientists do not always know when a volcano will erupt or how much damage it will cause. In the past, volcanoes have destroyed entire towns and killed thousands of people.

Creating islands

The Hawaiian Islands are made of basalt, but there were no violent eruptions involved in their formation. These islands formed as lava slowly leaked out of a **hotspot** – a place where magma spikes through the Earth's crust in the middle of a plate – and piled up over thousands of years. Eventually, the piles became tall enough to emerge from the surface of the ocean and form islands. Even today, new islands are being formed.

Old Faithful, a **geyser** in Yellowstone National Park in the USA, is fuelled by a hotspot. It erupts every thirty to ninety minutes, blasting steam and hot water up to 50 metres in the air.

THE FIVE DEADLIEST VOLCANOES IN HISTORY			
VOLCANO	NUMBER OF PEOPLE KILLED	LOCATION	DATE
Krakatoa	36,000	Java, Indonesia	1883
Pelée	28,000	Martinique	1902
Nevado del Ruiz	23,000	Armero, Colombia	1985
Etna	20,000	Sicily, Italy	1669
Vesuvius	16,000	Pompeii, Italy	AD 79

Cool as a crystal

You can see the crystals of feldspar, mica and quartz in granite. The red specks in this sample are made of feldspar.

DID YOU KNOW?

Gabbro and basalt are made of the same minerals – pyroxene, feldspar and olivine. They look different because gabbro cools more slowly and, therefore, has much larger crystals than basalt.

If you look closely at pieces of granite or gabbro, you can see their **crystals**. That's because the material that formed these igneous rocks did not spill out of **volcanoes** and cool quickly. Instead a pool of molten **magma** became trapped within the crust and cooled more slowly.

Most of the magma below the Earth's surface circulates slowly through the mantle. Each time magma gets close to the **core**, it is reheated. However, when magma is trapped at some depth underground, it eventually cools down and hardens to form igneous rock such as granite.

Even though the top of the mantle is much cooler than the bottom, it is still much warmer than the water or air at the Earth's surface. As a result, the **minerals** in igneous rock that forms below ground cool slowly over thousands of years. This gives the minerals time to form large, beautiful crystals.

Granite above ground

Now that you know gabbro and granite form underground, you may wonder why we see them on the surface today. Over time, the Earth's **tectonic plates** have moved, and rock that was once many miles below the surface is now exposed.

Land's End in Cornwall is made of granite, as are two huge, round boulders in Australia known as Devil's Marbles. These rocky structures formed deep underground and were later lifted above the Earth's surface. Over time, wind and water have worn away at their surfaces.

A MOUNTAIN-SIZED MEMORIAL

Between 1927 and 1941, American sculptor Gutzon Borglum used dynamite to help him carve out the faces of four famous US presidents on Mount Rushmore in the state of South Dakota. Today the 18-metre-tall sculptures of George Washington, Thomas Jefferson, Theodore Roosevelt and Abraham Lincoln can still be seen in the granite cliffs.

The rock cycle

Rocks are always changing. As **magma** cools to create new igneous rock, other kinds of rocks are being destroyed. You may think rock is indestructible, but over time, wind, water and ice can be even tougher.

Weathering

Crashing ocean waves, rivers, winds and glaciers can slowly wear away, or **erode**, even the hardest rock. Rocks can also be broken down when plant roots grow into cracks or crevices, when **acid rain** or snow falls. They might also break when they are repeatedly frozen and thawed or when living creatures release chemicals from their bodies. These changes are called **weathering**. Have you ever seen a boulder that looked like it had mysteriously split in half? The split was probably the result of weathering.

DID YOU KNOW?

Half Dome is a strangely shaped mountain at Yosemite National Park, California, USA. It is made of granodiorite – a kind of igneous rock. Half Dome was cut in half by an ice-age glacier moving across the land. On average, a glacier travels about 200 metres a year, but some move much faster.

Change over time

As rocks break down and wear away, the tiny pieces are picked up by rivers and streams. Eventually, some of these **sediments** travel all the way to the ocean. Over time, layers of deposited sediments build up and form **sedimentary rock**.

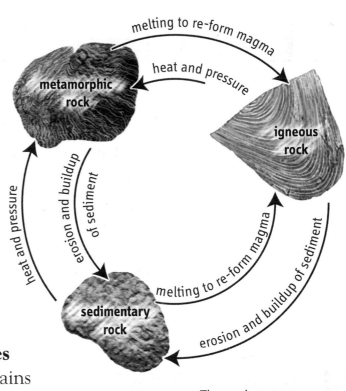

metamorphic rock

melting to re-form magma

heat and pressure

igneous rock

heat and pressure

erosion and buildup of sediment

melting to re-form magma

erosion and buildup of sediment

sedimentary rock

The Earth's **tectonic plates** may collide to form mountains and the sedimentary rocks become part of the land. When the layers are compressed, the sedimentary rock is exposed to tremendous heat and pressure. Over millions of years, the sedimentary rock may change into **metamorphic rock**. The rock may be heated so much that it will melt and become magma. Eventually, some of that magma will cool to form igneous rock once more.

The rock we see on the Earth today has not always been here. Rock forms and breaks down in a never-ending cycle.

SEE FOR YOURSELF

The next time you visit the seaside pick up some pebbles along the beach. Compare them to pebbles you find in your garden or in a local park. The edges of the pebbles from the seaside will be rounder and smoother than land pebbles because water has worn them down. Seaside pebbles show erosion at work.

Where on Earth is igneous rock?

Sugar Loaf Mountain is a famous landmark in Rio de Janeiro, Brazil. It was exposed as wind and water eroded the softer rock around it.

DID YOU KNOW?

The oldest known rock in the world was found in 1986 near Perth in Western Australia. It is at least 4.4 billion years old.

Igneous rocks are the most common rocks in the Earth's **crust**. For example, the seabed is made of volcanic basalt. The Andes Mountains in South America are made of andesite. This volcanic mountain range has slowly risen as the Nazca Plate crashes into the American Plate (see the map on page 8). Black sand beaches in Iceland, Scotland, New Zealand and Greece are all made of tiny grains of igneous rock that came from **volcanoes**.

Some of the most incredible rock formations in the world are made of igneous rock that formed deep underground. Hay Tor in Devon in the UK and Sugar Loaf Mountain in Brazil formed when wind and water gradually wore away all the surrounding rock.

There are many ancient legends that try to explain how the Giant's Causeway in Northern Ireland formed. Today we know its step-like columns are made of basalt. As the rock is slowly **eroded** by the sea, it breaks into blocks that look like a huge staircase. Le Puy de Dôme in France is also made of igneous rock. It was once the central part of a volcano, but the surrounding rock slowly eroded over time.

Obsidian formations

Obsidian, a shiny volcanic igneous rock, is usually only found in small amounts. However, giant rock formations known as the Glass Buttes in Oregon, USA and the Valles Caldera in the US state of New Mexico are made entirely of obsidian.

DID YOU KNOW?

According to an ancient Native American legend, a group of girls was chased by an angry bear, so they ran as far as they could and then climbed up a rock where they hoped they would be safe. As the huge, ferocious bear jumped and clawed at its sides, the rock grew taller and taller to protect the girls. The rock, which Northern Plains tribes called Bear's Lodge, was considered a sacred site. In 1906, US President Theodore Roosevelt declared the 386-metre-tall basalt rock one of the first American national monuments. Located in the state of Wyoming, it is now known as Devils Tower. Scientists believe that it is the core of an ancient volcano.

Igneous rocks in space

The Moon is made entirely of igneous rock. The highlands – the areas that look white from the Earth – are made of anorthosite, norite and troctolite. The Moon's dark patches, or marias, are made of basalt.

About ten billion years ago, a giant, spinning cloud of dust and hot gases began to form in our galaxy, the Milky Way. Eventually, a brightly glowing ball formed at the centre of the cloud. That ball was the Sun. As more time passed, some of the remaining dust and gases began clumping together. As these larger objects hurtled through space, they collided with one another and slowly grew even bigger.

Planet formation

Eventually, a few very large objects formed our solar system. Close to the Sun, four small planets with rocky surfaces formed – Mercury, Venus, Earth and Mars. The upper layers of the other rocky planets are made of igneous rock, like on the Earth. Many moons, including the Earth's Moon, are made entirely of igneous rock.

DID YOU KNOW?

Chondrites are the oldest known rocks in the solar system. These meteorites, made of igneous rock, formed about 4.6 billion years ago.

This incredible image of Asteroid 243 Ida was taken by the Hubble Space Telescope. It is 58 kilometres (36 miles) long and has many craters on its surface.

Further out in the solar system, four planets known as 'gas giants' formed – Jupiter, Saturn, Uranus and Neptune. These planets have gaseous surfaces with solid cores and are made of some of the same materials as the rocky planets.

Each year, about 19,000 bits of rock from space strike the Earth. Most of these **meteorites** are too small to be noticed. But sometimes scientists find football-sized meteorites on the ice in Antarctica, which they can study. Meteorites are often made of igneous rock. Many meteorites from Mars are made of pyroxenite. Some rocky chunks that have broken off from **asteroids** are made of pallasite.

UP CLOSE AND PERSONAL

In the late 1960s and 1970s, a dozen American astronauts visited the Moon. Most of them had been trained as pilots, but Harrison 'Jack' Schmitt was a geologist – a scientist who studies rocks and rock formations. During his *Apollo 17* mission, Schmitt observed the Moon's surface firsthand to try to understand how the moon formed and how it has changed over time. Later, he described what he saw to other scientists.

How do people use igneous rock?

The walls of the Empire State Building in New York City are made of granite. Granite is an important building material because it is very durable.

People use igneous rock in many ways. For example, most of the roads and car parks in the United States are paved with crushed basalt because it is common and durable. Basalt is also used in many places to build road curbs. The world-famous Moai statues at Anakena Beach on Easter Island in the Pacific are built from basalt. These giant structures, carved to look like human heads and upper bodies, were constructed by native peoples more than 400 years ago.

Building with granite

Granite is a very popular building material. Its strength and beauty make it a good choice for sculptures, gravestones and buildings. The walls of the Empire State Building in New York City are made of white granite. So are the towers at each end of the Sydney Harbour Bridge in New South Wales, Australia. Tower Bridge in London is built of grey granite from Cornwall.

Volcanic glass

Obsidian is a fast-cooling **volcanic** glass. It is usually pure black, but may also be brown or black with shiny bands of purple, green and gold.

In the past, Native American people used it to make tools and weapons, such as arrowheads. Because it has such tiny **crystals**, obsidian is hard and flakes easily for shaping. Other groups of early people used it to make masks, mirrors and jewellery. Obsidian is also used in some places to decorate stone buildings because it is pure black, shiny and easy to shape.

Obsidian is an igneous rock. Because it is hard and chips easily, it has been used to make weapons by many peoples.

Amazing igneous rocks

Have you ever found a little rock in the pocket of a new pair of jeans? That rock was probably pumice. Jeans are sometimes washed with pumice to give them a faded look. Pumice, an igneous rock, is the lightest rock on the Earth. The holes you see in pumice are filled with air that was trapped when the lava it was made from cooled quickly.

Pumice is so lightweight it can float in water. This igneous rock is an important ingredient in many household cleaners.

Diamond in the rock

Pumice is not the only special igneous rock. Many people would like to find kimberlite. But they aren't as interested in the kimberlite as they are in what may be found near by – diamonds and other valuable gems. Large, beautiful **crystals** often form in and around kimberlite as the rock slowly cools.

ODOUR EATERS

A small company in Billings, in the US state of Montana, is selling volcanic rocks from a local quarry as natural odour removers. No one knows exactly how they work, but they are popular.

The company ships 30 tonnes a month to destinations throughout the world. The rocks remove odours for two to four weeks and can be 'recharged' by placing them out in the Sun for two days.

Amazing volcanic rocks

Pele's Hair is the name used to describe long, golden filaments of obsidian. These hairlike structures sometimes form when lava spurts from a **volcano**, is caught by the wind, and then cools in long, glassy strands before it hits the ground. If you saw Pele's Hair, you would probably never guess that it is a type of igneous rock. It certainly doesn't look like it!

When volcanic rocks, such as rhyolite, basalt or andesite, cool quickly, large gas bubbles are trapped and appear as holes inside them. As time passes, these cavities may fill with large quartz crystals, such as amethyst, or with beautifully banded agate. Artists in ancient Greece and Rome often carved beautiful cameos from agate.

DID YOU KNOW?

Tourists who visit Crater of Diamonds State Park in Arkansas, USA can use the spades and sifting trays provided to hunt for kimberlite and diamonds. Anything that is found can be taken away by the visitors.

Identifying igneous rocks

No matter where you live, you see dozens of rocks every day. They are in your house, in the walls of buildings and on the ground. You've probably never paid too much attention to these rocks, but take a closer look. Some of them may be igneous rocks.

Rocks from lava

Knowing where a rock comes from can help you identify it. For example, if a rock came from a place where there was once – or still is – an active **volcano**, then it is probably igneous rock – especially if it is smooth and glassy or hard and black.

Sometimes lava spreads out in great sheets and covers very large areas of land. An area in Western Victoria in Australia, known as the Great Basalt Plains, is now a grassland habitat, but it formed millions of years ago as a very large sheet of lava cooled.

Basalt is the most common kind of igneous rock. It often forms six-sided columns when the rock cools and then fractures.

IMAGINE THAT!

Igneous rocks can tell a geologist where **magma** spilled onto the land thousands of years ago. For many years, scientists believed that the mountains in the Cascade Range in Washington, USA were volcanic because they found many samples of igneous rock in the area. When one of the mountains, Mount St Helens (left), erupted in 1980, researchers were not surprised that it was a volcano.

To find out even more about a rock, you can study its **crystals**. Most rocks with medium or large crystals are igneous rocks that formed underground. Igneous rocks that formed when lava cooled have much smaller crystals.

A rock's colour, texture, shininess and hardness can also help you identify the **minerals** in it. In general, igneous rocks have a uniform texture and evenly distributed colours. Many igneous rocks contain minerals such as quartz, feldspar, olivine, pyroxene, biotite and musovite mica, and amphibole. These minerals tend to be fairly hard.

Of course, one of the best ways to identify a rock is to study a field guide to rocks and minerals. These books show pictures of rocks and give detailed descriptions of them.

Rock collecting

Now that you have learned how to identify igneous rocks, would you like to collect some? You can buy all kinds of beautiful and interesting igneous rock samples. You can also view them at a natural history museum, but it might be more fun to hunt for them in local parks, in fields or in the woods.

These students are collecting rocks on a school field trip. Do you think the sample they are observing is igneous rock?

Before you begin planning your first rock hunting trip, you will need to gather together a few pieces of equipment. You will also need to learn a few simple, but important, rules.

DID YOU KNOW?

Rock and **mineral** clubs are very popular all over the world. These clubs sponsor exhibits, organize field trips and may even help build museum collections. By joining a club, you can also meet other people who are interested in rocks.

Be systematic!

Once you have identified the rocks, you may want to create a system for labelling, organizing and storing them. Then you will always be able to find a specific sample later.

You can arrange your specimens any way you like – by colour, by crystal shape, by collection site or even alphabetically. As your collection grows, being organized will become more and more important.

You can store your rock collection in a cardboard box. Be sure to label the individual specimens.

WHAT YOU NEED TO KNOW

- Never go rock hunting alone. Go with a group that includes a qualified adult.
- Know how to use a map and compass.
- Always get a landowner's permission before walking on private property. If you find interesting rocks, ask the owner if you can remove them.
- Before removing samples from public land, make sure rock collecting is allowed. Many natural rock formations are protected by law.
- Respect nature. Do not hammer out samples. Do not disturb living things and do not leave litter.

WHAT YOU NEED

- Strong boots or wellies
- A map and compass
- A small paintbrush to clean dirt and extra rock chips off the samples
- A camera to take photographs of rock formations
- A hand lens to get a close-up look at the rocks
- A notebook for recording when and where you find each rocks
- A spotter's guide to rocks and minerals.

Glossary

acid rain rain that is polluted with acid in the atmosphere and that damages the environment

asteroid chunk of rock that orbits the Sun within the solar system

atom smallest unit of an element that has all of the properties of that element

cameo piece of jewellery or picture that usually features a human head carved in relief

core centre of the Earth. The inner core is solid, and the outer core is liquid.

crust outer layer of the Earth

crystal repeating structure within most minerals

erode to slowly wear away rock over time by the action of wind, water or glaciers

face smooth, flat side of a crystal

geyser kind of hot spring that occasionally spews steam and hot water

hotspot place in the middle of a tectonic plate where magma spikes through the Earth's crust

magma hot, liquid rock that makes up the Earth's mantle. When magma spills out onto the Earth's surface, it is called lava.

mantle layer of the Earth between the crust and outer core. It is made of rock in its liquid form, known as magma.

metamorphic rock kind of rock that forms when heat or pressure changes the minerals within igneous rock, sedimentary rock or another metamorphic rock

meteorite chunk of rock from space that hits the Earth or another object in space

mineral natural solid material with a specific chemical makeup and structure

molecule smallest unit of a substance, made up of one or more atoms

property trait or characteristic that helps make identification possible

rift crack in the Earth's surface created when two tectonic plates move away from each other

seafloor spreading process that occurs when the Earth's plates move apart, creating a long crack on the seabed

sediment mud, clay or bits of rock picked up by rivers and streams and dumped in the ocean

sedimentary rock kind of rock formed as layers of mud, clay, tiny rocks and other materials build up over time

tectonic plate one of the large slabs of rock that make up the Earth's crust

transform fault crack that forms on the Earth's surface where two tectonic plates scrape against each other

volcano opening in the Earth's surface that extends down into the mantle

weathering breaking down of rock by plant roots or by repeated freezing and thawing

Further information

BOOKS

The Kingfisher book of planet Earth, Martin Redfern, Kingfisher, 1999

The pebble in my pocket, Meredith Hopper, Frances Lincoln, 1997

The best book of fossils, rocks and minerals, Chris Pellant, Kingfisher, 2000

Tourists rock, fossil and mineral map of Great Britain, British Geological Survey, 2000

ORGANIZATIONS

British Geological Survey
www.bgs.ac.uk
Kingsley Dunham Centre, Keyworth, Nottingham, NG12 5GG
UK

Rockwatch
www.geologist.demon.co.uk/rockwatch/
The Geologists' Association
Burlington House, Piccadilly, London, W1V 9AG
UK

The Natural History Museum
www.nhm.ac.uk
Cromwell Road,
London, SW7 5BD
UK

The Geological Society of Australia
www.gsa.org.au/home
Suite 706, 301 George Street
Sydney NSW 2000
Australia

Geological Survey of Canada
www.nrcan.gc.ca/gsc/
601 Booth Street
Ottawa, Ontario
KIA 0E8
Canada

US Geological Survey (USGS)
www.usgs.gov
507 National Center
12201 Sunrise Valley Drive
Reston, Virginia 22092
USA

Index

Igneous Rocks

Melissa Stewart

www.heinemann.co.uk/library
Visit our website to find out more information about Heinemann Library books.

To order:
☎ Phone 44 (0) 1865 888066
🖹 Send a fax to 44 (0) 1865 314091
💻 Visit the Heinemann Bookshop at www.heinemann.co.uk/library to browse our catalogue and order online.

First published in Great Britain by Heinemann Library, Halley Court, Jordan Hill, Oxford OX2 8EJ
a division of Reed Educational and Professional Publishing Ltd. Heinemann is a registered trademark
of Reed Educational and Professional Publishing Ltd.

OXFORD MELBOURNE AUCKLAND JOHANNESBURG BLANTYRE
GABORONE IBADAN PORTSMOUTH (NH) USA CHICAGO

Produced for Heinemann Library by Editorial Directions
Designed by Ox and Company
Originated by Ambassador Litho Ltd
Printed in China

ISBN 0 431 14372 2 (hardback)   ISBN 0 431 14380 3 (paperback)
06 05 04 03 02   07 06 05 04 03
10 9 8 7 6 5 4 3 2 1   10 9 8 7 6 5 4 3 2 1

British Library Cataloguing in Publication Data
Stewart, Melissa
  Igneous rocks. – (Rocks and minerals)
  1. Rocks, Igneous – Juvenile literature
  I. Title
  552.1

Acknowledgements
The Publishers would like to thank the following for permission to reproduce photographs:

Photographs ©: Cover, Bob Daemmrich/The Image Works; p. 4, James P. Rowan; p. 5, R.W. Gerling/Visuals Unlimited, Inc.;
p. 7, Vince Streano/Corbis; p. 10 top, David Johnson/Reed Consumer Books, Ltd.; p. 10 bottom, A.J. Copley/Visuals
Unlimited, Inc.; p. 11, Lysbeth Corsi/Visuals Unlimited, Inc.; p. 12, Joe Carini/The Image Works; p. 13, Fritz Polking/Visuals
Unlimited, Inc.; p. 14, Adam Smith/FPG International; p. 15, James P. Rowan; p. 16, Dean Conger/Corbis; p. 17, Jeff
Greenberg/The Image Works; p. 18, Cameramann International, Ltd.; p. 19, Corbis; p. 20, Jack K. Clark/The Image Works;
p. 21, Gamma Liaison/Hulton Archive; p. 22, Grace Davies Photography; p. 23, James L. Amos/Corbis; p. 24, Dane S.
Johnson/Visuals Unlimited, Inc.; p. 25, Buddy Mays/Corbis; p. 26, Tess Young/Tom Stack & Associates; p. 27, Corbis; pp. 28,
29, Daemmrich/The Image Works.

Every effort has been made to contact copyright holders of any material reproduced in this book. Any omissions will be
rectified in subsequent printings if notice is given to the Publishers.

Our thanks to Alan Timms and Martin Lawrence of the Natural History Museum, London for their assistance in the
preparation of this edition.